Perfectly Imperfect

By
Mecheal Elizabeth

Conscious Dreams
PUBLISHING

Copyright © 2024: Mecheal Elizabeth

All rights reserved. No part of this publication may be produced, distributed, or transmitted in any form or by any means, including photocopying, recording, or other electronic or mechanical methods, without the prior written permission of the publisher, except in the case of brief quotations embodied in critical reviews and certain other non-commercial uses permitted by copyright law.

Published by Conscious Dreams Publishing
www.consciousdreamspublishing.com

Edited by Daniella Blechner

Typeset by Nadia Vitushynska

ISBN: 978-1-915522-75-7

DEDICATION

In loving memory of Alexander Paul.
Your bright spiritual soul inspired me
to write my first poem.

As a spoken word poet, he was phenomenal.
His poem
'I AM'
had the most profound effect on me.
I could neither read nor watch his YouTube video without tears.
I am truly blessed to have known you and your mother
who persevered through her grief to bring his work to light.

Thank you

CONTENTS

The Unveiling 7
- Appearance 8
- Plummet 9
- Brother's Wish 11
- Today 12
- In 3s 13
- Shut Doors 14
- Scared 15
- The Bench Table 16
- Black Reality 18
- Your Smile 20
- Love Would 22
- Pain 24
- Up Close and Personal 26
- Waiting 27
- Too Tired 28

The Psychologist 29
- A Conversation 30
- The Meeting 32
- What a Someting 33
- When Time Stood Still 34
- Picture That 36
- Settled 37
- Too Strong 38
- Crushed 39
- '55' Wow !! 40
- Whilst We Are Here 41

- Lord Give Me Strength 42
- Refresh 43
- Life On Lockdown 44
- Park of Discovery 45
- How Many Times? 47
- Give Me 48
- Am I Grateful 49
- The Purge 51
- You 52
- Me 54
- God's Plan 55

The Light 57
- Beautiful Bird 58
- Night Out 59
- Glitch 60
- Memories 61
- Calm 62
- Noise 63
- Feet 64
- Space 66
- Life Lights 67
- Everything 69
- The Brave 70
- The Canvas 71
- Water 73
- Nature Is Perfectly Imperfect 74

About the Author 75
Acknowledgements 77

The Lord will guide you always; he will satisfy your needs
in the sun-scorched land and will strengthen your frame.
You will be like a well-watered garden
like a spring whose waters never fail.

Isaiah 58:11

The Unveiling

In the same way, the Spirit helps us in our weakness.
We do not know what we ought to pray for,
but the Spirit himself intercedes for us
through wordless groans…

Romans 8:26

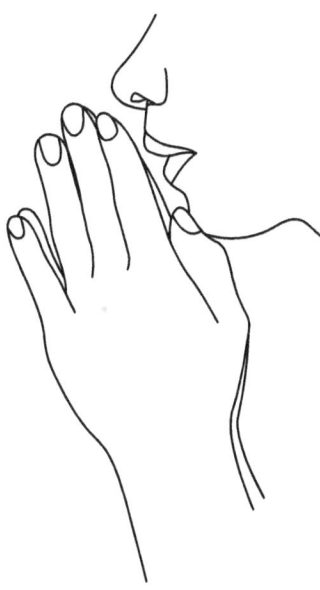

APPEARANCE

Not because you cannot see
Don't believe it's not happening
Not because you see a smile and laughter
Don't believe they're not crying
Not because they do something nice
Don't believe they are not hurting
Not because you see kindness
There's no sadness
Not because you see peace
A storm, a hurricane hasn't rampaged through them
Not because you can feel stillness
A tornado has not twisted a beating heart
Leaving them weak and destitute; lonely in the dark
Not because you cannot see
Don't believe it's all love

PLUMMET

Plummet and vomit
That's my world
A sick feeling of doom
Where nothing seems to bloom
The world is full of doom and gloom
Cascading from one disaster to another
Where is the optimistic outlook of our life
The angel of good grace
Where is the founder of electrifying energy
That allows us to plug in at the source
And shock us into a life worth living
The natural order says we will pass on someday
I want to live life before it comes my way
I want to lose that downward smile and
Start to fly high above the clouds
My world as I knew it shattered into tiny little pieces
Pieces of lies

Kinks in my road—unable to straighten these out
I now cast it aside
Rebuilding the life worth living has confused me to no end
Anxiety has taken hold
I tremble under the weight of my many thoughts
Of what to do
I'm afraid to ask the question
Who are you?
Oops, that sick feeling is back again
As the nerves rise within my system

It has taken all my strength to hold it down
As I took a long, hard look at myself in the mirror
Unpicking the faults, the cause of numerous situations
I camouflage my feelings with smiles
Praying and hoping it will all be fine
But at this time, I choose to sit in this space
Waiting for God to show me grace

BROTHER'S WISH

I wish I could fall in love
I wish I could love myself for the things I can and cannot do
I wish I wish I wish I could
Do the things I know I should

My brothers, they do care for me
My sister, she loves me too
My mother, she says prayers all night
I hope that things will be all right
My daddy doesn't know what to say
He's at a loss all day
I've dug a hole so deep I don't know what to do or say
Can't see how you all still love me the same way
I cannot forgive myself for what I've said and done
I won't go and face anyone
I'm losing every part of me ever so slowly
Oh, how I feel so really lonely
My children love me
But now they don't want to know me
I've let them down when they needed me
I'm so sorry, I feel I'm no good

I wish I wish I wish I could stop doing what I'm doing
And hold on to a prayer
I'm scared, fighting to take that leap of faith
'Cause I'm empty and my mind is not all there
I wish I wish I wish I could believe in what I really should
But the myrrh has got me good
I wish I wish I wish I could love myself the way I should

TODAY

Today I woke without much vigour
No strength to call my own
My spirit dipped and plummeted so low
I really could say goodbye and go
I don't know why I feel this way
I smiled through all my pain each day
My body said it had enough and my mind just got
Into a rut
Every part of me seems to hurt
My temperament is now curt
The medication, I pray to work
Relieve me from this pain
I've left it till the last minute
So I can try and get some sleep
I've massaged and rubbed the tender parts
They feel like painful darts
I pray God blesses me, and I give thanks for another day
And hope my pain someday will go away

IN 3S

My telly has gone on the blink
The screen has gone all blank
My heating has gone to pastures new
So now I experience Iceland and not Cancún
My computer refused to let me live vicariously
It took away all my dreams
Sending me back to the flooded floor
So I could complain some more
They say things happens in threes
So I waited for something else to go wrong
The telly was the third bad thing
So now I can breathe and sing once more
Oh, dear I just realised it was actually four

SHUT DOORS

Shut doors say I've had enough
Shut doors say I've cut you off
Shut doors say I don't want to see you
Shut doors say I cannot please you
Shut doors say there is no compromise
They don't tell me why
There's no discussion or dialogue
Of what's hidden deep inside
When doors are open it says
You're welcome
It invites a calm spirit and mind
Which is open to endless possibilities
And agreements in time
Whether or not to agree
Or agree to disagree
Your position is fully discussed
I cannot explore this if the door is shut first

SCARED

I am scared to expose myself to thee
To show my vulnerability
Scared of getting my feelings hurt
Receiving scathing, savaging comments on my work
Which may send my soul deeper underground
Truth be told, I really want to share my stories poems
My thoughts, I do despair
My ideas they bubble in a stewpot
With a multitude of ingredients, it differs with every taste
Waiting to be sampled, not in haste
This pot should not be rushed
For I may receive a nasty burn
The pain may be too much for me to contemplate
Returning to that stewpot once again
Be brave, my mind is telling me
My heart is slow to follow
Do not invest in negativity then sabotage your own creativity
As long as you are coming from a place of love
Be yourself and do your stuff

THE BENCH TABLE

This bench table is a symbol of what I have become to you
Pure and untainted wood
Now repurposed and put together by you
A beautiful piece waiting to shine through the mist
You carefully assembled the pieces
Primed the wood and carefully painted
Your goal, you finally achieved it
Then, one day, your spirit is disturbed
Uncompromising you, systematically destroying
The very thing you say you loved and appreciated
With so many impulsive impatient strokes
Of mindless blunders, jealousy
Rage and insecurity just because
Notwithstanding the damage you cause
Forgiveness comes freely from me
And the bench table is repaired yet again
And just when you think you can take a seat
And enjoy the summer morning sun
Your mood changes and a splash of paint is thrown all over
It is damaged once again
The cycle is repeated so many times, damage and repairs
Until I can no longer enjoy the seat
I wait for some travesty to occur
Uncertain if I should ever be here at all
I question my sense and sensibility
Can I not see a pattern?
Is this love or codependency?
Like the bench table, I am still out in the cold

Broken with deep cuts that may never heal at all
I am just weathering the storms
Yet every year, the bench table gets a different coat of paint
More vibrant than last season's efforts
Not knowing, all the time, a roaring fire of resentment
Burns deep within your furnace
Unable to be contained or reached to be put out
My efforts, my love, seemed so futile
I didn't know such feelings were in the mix
I did not read the signs
But I always knew something was amiss
Something was just not right
So I turn my mind to the one who is here to save
And pray that He will gather all my pain
And put it neatly away

BLACK REALITY

When I close my eyes at night
My fear is not that I won't wake up
My fear is that I will wake up
Realise I am still stuck in a world that is really messed up
Still struggling to have that necessary conversation with my son
On why a Black man was killed by a racist knee
Just because he was Black, like you and me

Warn him about the dangers of life
Tell him that it's because he's not white
Tell him that racism is rife
And show him the reality of the kind
Who seeks to demoralise our Black mind
Show the atrocities being committed
Educate him on race and civil liberties

Having guided him on the laws of the land
And helping him reach his full potential
Tell him that even when he's at the top of his game
And he shakes his white peers' hands
He must be aware that they don't see him as equal
Just because he is a Black man

It's sad to see
This should not be such a consideration
Yes, your race, the colour of your face
Can invoke such prejudice and hatred from another nation

The Unveiling

My son, I'm sorry but it's true
There's not much that you can do
Be aware of who you are, your strengths, and
Hold true to the value you possess
Stand proud and smile
You are a beautiful creature, you are well blessed
Educate yourself
And know how to navigate the evil flaws of human nature

YOUR SMILE

I am embarrassed by your smile
I never thought it would come to this
Not a word or a stolen kiss
You turn my world upside down
I can't have any more of this
Whatever you think this is
I am so embarrassed when you smile
You're the reason why I cry
How can you say you love me now
When all you want to do is to tear me down
Your words not mine
They cut so deep
Now I cannot even sleep
Then you put a smile upon your face
And seek to want a warm embrace
I'm so embarrassed by your smile
While all the time it hides your many resentments
Deep inside
What a fool I've been for so long
I've questioned everything you've ever said and done
You've made me question my reality
And that's not me doubting all I see
I've gone down a road of negativity
When I only deal with positivity
I am embarrassed by your smile
'Cause I have held your secrets too long inside
Breathe deep, I tell myself
Keep your spirits up and get some help

So I call upon my spiritual angels above to intercede
On my behalf. I wasn't sure
If God would make time to speak with me

I finally hear a whisper:
'You can do all things through Christ who strengthens thee'
It's tough right now, but they'll soon be gone
Come to me, just you alone
Pain knows pain; I'll bring you through
Trust me—I have a new plan for you
All you have to do is come hold my hand
Now you will never be embarrassed by my smile
I will always love you and be your guide
Protect you—I'll be by your side
You are and always have been a blessed child; a child of God
So step into my house and receive my precious blood

LOVE WOULD

When you left her that morning
Did you check that she was still breathing
Knowing that you'd not see her for the next twelve hours?
Love would have checked
Love would have stopped to care
Love would not have left without saying a prayer
When you left her that morning
A simple kiss would have sufficed
To ensure the revival of the heart brought back to life
If she'd died that morning, what would you have said?
I saw her last night, just before I went to bed?
I grunted goodnight with my heart full of anger
My soul full of bitterness
My mind full of resentment and displeasure?
What would you have told them
About this poor, displeasing wife?
How she was so awful
And how she didn't cook you dinner that night?
So you left her that morning without saying a single word
You left her for dead and continued moaning
There's no need to moan any more
She is finally out your life, which is just going right
There is no one hindering your plans
Go get it
Grab life with open hands
Did you ever stop to wonder?
You were free to do this anyway
It was your fears, impatience and narcissistic ways

That kept you in your position
You made her the object of your frustration and pain
Unable to channel your love in a positive and loving way
Be thankful now
Joy cometh in the morning
Be happy now, be hopeful and enjoy your purpose
There is no one else now to blame
For the choices you wish to make

Blessed is he who takes heed of mistakes made in their past
I pray that there will be forgiveness on both parts
And your blessing will come at last

PAIN

Pain a subjective experience
One that is hard to compare
Each person has a comparable relationship
So different in every way
Don't tell me you understand my pain
You can hardly tell unless I spell it out
Oblivious to my endurance level
Tested to extremity
When is it going to end?
My pressure rises to levels of concern
Yet I say nothing
I wait and breathe it out
Sometimes taking a pill or two
Hoping it will go unnoticed too
I don't want to concern you all
It's my pain not yours
I just have to manage it now
But pain is taking its toll
Can't sleep at night
My days are really sore
Skin touched
It is pricked with sharp darts of pain once more
My body battered from sustained warfare yet again
My face, my eyes—my mouth reflects an upside down smile
Finding it hard to straighten this out this time
Yet all I hear is berating tones and wailing sounds of failures
Pain is a debilitating feature you cannot begin to imagine
Those fortunate not to have this constant nemesis
They really cannot empathise

The Unveiling

No one wants to hang their pain on the line there for all to see
To take potshots at their credibility
Is she really feeling it or making much of nothing?
Can't be bothered by those thoughts
I can't and won't take it on
Not because I'm still pushing on
Don't think it's not happening or that it's even gone

Pain, my constant companion and foe
Can bring you down so very, very low
So when you see a smile on my face
And hear laughter in the air
That's the day I am blessed by grace
Whose sympathy is always there

UP CLOSE AND PERSONAL

Up close and personal, what do you see
A quizzical eye
A mystique wonder
Hoping to ponder the mind of the beauty that cannot speak
Intent is well meant, but fear generates a swift and hasty retreat
Regardless of the language you speak
A cacophony of endless sound bites is extended
Rendering you powerless, unable to communicate with me
You let another influence and destroy your choice of words
Curb your thoughts and plant seeds that no longer flourish
Nor encourage you to grow
Now in the middle of this difficulty, there lies an opportunity
To challenge and change the status quo
But you hang on to what you know
Even though it no longer serves you or makes you whole
I cannot hold your hand in that journey
It's going in the wrong direction
My light is too bright to be covered up by your night
So I ask God to take control
You may not understand the power of the spirit
But I know where my help comes from
He knows the plans he has for me
Plans to make me prosper
Plans that will not harm me
I wish you well no matter what has passed
Hoping you will find peace at last

WAITING

I'm waiting for a break in life
Where wisdom outplays trouble and strife
A solid walk of stability
A seldom peace retreat
To revive my heart, my health, my strength
My self-belief
In the Creator's vision set out for me
The gift of life is life itself
The ultimate prize given here on earth

TOO TIRED

Too tired to talk
Too tired to walk
Too tired to smile
Too tired to cry
Too tired to breathe
Too tired to grieve
Too tired to believe that anything can be achieved
Then one day an agreement is made
To change and invigorate you again
To hope that life is worth living once more
As there are so many things to applaud
Count your blessings, one by one
At least you are here that's number one

The Psychologist

Trust in the Lord with all your heart and lean
not on your own understanding; in all your ways submit
to Him and He will make your path straight.

Proverbs 3:5

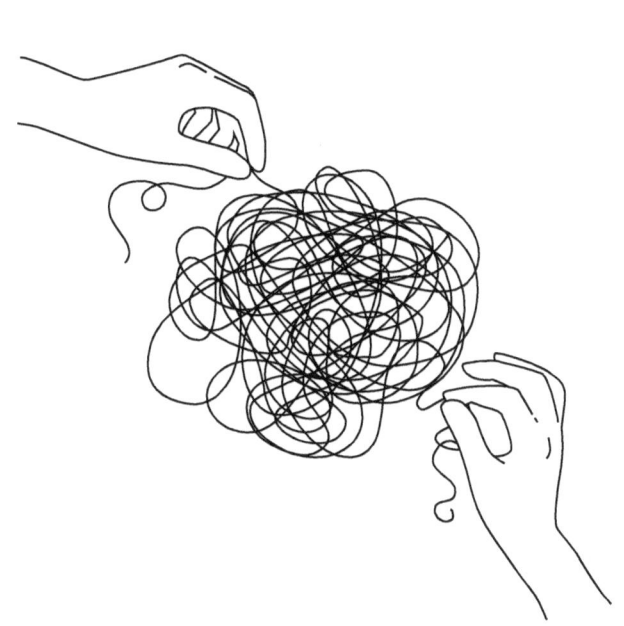

A CONVERSATION

It starts with a conversation
A truthful, honest conversation
The utterance of those first words
Sets the tone of what is to follow
Conjure in the mind the assemblance of an aura
Capable of conveying the right message to the receiver

Again, I say it starts with a conversation
A visual presentation
The eyes, the facial lines, have now connected
In ways so unexpected
A lot is said, maybe too much
Which may be at cross purposes with the conversation

It starts with a conversation
Your body speaks before your breath has carried a word
It said so much; it offended the receivers
Unintentionally, the message is now lost

It starts with a conversation
A conversation with you
Have you set the tone with yourself
And looked at the conversation in the mirror?
Is it what you intended? Make sure you come correct
Is it what you want it to look like and what you expected?

The conversation has now begun
The delivery is what you planned
The message you have now sent
Has somehow gone off-plan
The spoken words do not correspond with your intention
The mind is now racing to catch up
Not foreseeing the obvious prediction
That when you speak without carefully
Analysing or considering your own position
Your message, however good it was intended
Can be lost by its method of transportation

THE MEETING

When my heart meets my soul
Will it recognise its host?
When my heart meets my soul
Will rejection be its choice?
When my heart meets my soul
Will there be mutual love and affection?
Will the soul welcome my heart or
Sever all connections?
When my heart meets my soul
Will my body come alive
Loving what it sees, leaping to the sky?
When my heart meets my soul
Will it request the pleasure of a dance
A dance of mutual harmony
Not torment fear or acrimony?
When my heart meets my soul
Will it say unto thee
Soul to heart, please forgive me?

WHAT A SOMETING

Aging; what a somet'ing
I can't even read my own handwriting
Without glasses this evening
The ageing process began a long time ago
I just didn't realise
I just didn't know
One day I looked in the mirror
Someone looked back at me
I picked up my glasses
I needed to see
I think it was the real me
My eyes had lost its glint
My face started to squint

The moustache said hello
The hairs on my chin gave a wink
I barely move without a twinge
Yes it started, and it's not gonna go
Till you're six foot under then
There is no more hellos
Although I hear they say your nails still
Continue to grow
So I better make sure they are well-manicured and painted so
I can leave them on show

Jokes aside, I cannot be too concerned with age
I'll just make sure that I lead a happy fulfilled life instead

WHEN TIME STOOD STILL

When time stood still
Where was your mind?
When time rushed by
Where was I?
When time had true good meaning
How, really, am I?
Frozen still in time
Whether good, bad or pensive
Show me what I am
Am I a floating leaf in the sky
Riding the light breeze
Landing wherever the wind takes
Me across the seas?
My mind reflects an image
It said, don't look at me I am not here
Really
I'm lost, an empty bottle waiting to be filled
With smiles and laughter
A basket full of joyful euphoria
Not dragged down with the weights of life
I'm not the person I ought to be
I'm not the person I want to be
What is she supposed to, ought to, should be?
It's a long time since I've looked deeply
Having difficulty surfacing the true me
A hatchet job, a mosaic of unwanted pieces of life
A magnet attracting an abundance of anything
Like an eclipse of the sun, I cover my eyes

The Psychologist

Never wanting see what's really inside
In that instant, it is revealed to me
How economical I am with the truth of me
Not as strong as people see me
Now I am willing to take steps to break free
To unveil and reveal the true me

PICTURE THAT

At times I wait to see
What visions come before me
I close my eyes and focus gently
On the darkness so intently
Then, slowly, a picture appears through
Streams of perfect light
Forming an image, a sight for sore eyes
What do I see? What does this really mean to me?
Can it be translated by this visionary?
Can my art determine what it's gonna be
Or will the picture fade inside of me
Never to be seen?

SETTLED

I have settled for so long
I don't know where my happiness begins
I have settled for so much
I struggled for freedom
I have settled for inadequate positions
That could never be sustained
I have settled for so little and nothing I have gained
Not recognising my true value within my frame
That which I have settled for has been
My real undoing
So, I say I will not settle anymore
I'm more deserving, for sure
I will not settle to be second best
First place, I say, or not at all
I will not settle and go quietly
I will not be ignored
I will not make excuses for lack of respect
Or rudeness I have endured as part of the course
I'll dress my best and love me as I should be
Claim back my integrity
And be who my spirit tells me to be
As imperfect as I am, I'll settle anymore 'cause
I deserve to be happy, once and for all

TOO STRONG

Don't be too strong when weakness is needed
Don't be too strong when crying is needed
Don't be too strong when, clearly, help is needed
Just don't be too strong
Don't let your strength become your weakness
'Cause your pride has taken pride of place
Where, clearly, it's not needed
Strength comes from not being a martyr
It's about relinquishing control and having confidence in another
When you are unable to cope in light of your struggles
Don't be too strong; it can be your undoing,
Be gracious and accept. Just be grateful for receiving
Don't be too strong that you turn your angels away
Or turn down someone
Who just wants to do their good deed for the day
Don't be too strong that you kick a gift horse in the mouth
Be grateful for every blessing you are to and will receive
Without a doubt
Surrender to the plethora of abundance
And express gratitude throughout
You are deserving of the pure love
That God just keeps giving out

CRUSHED

I've crushed up so many papers up and thrown them in the bin
My thoughts, my pain, my expectations
And all my feelings within
I've laid bare my discontented soul, which now needs healing
So, today, I've decided it's another day
No more paper torn to shreds and thrown away
I'll now stick my heart together
And believe that all I have been through
Will be worth it in the end
Got my pen, my faithful friend
I'll not allow another word to enter my head
That degrades and says I'm worthless
I need no one's approval
To say you've done real good
This approval I've now taken away and carefully put in storage
I've lived more years than I have have left
So time is of the essence to show what I can do
I love myself, my family
I'm bright and giving, too
I am carefully choosing who receives my strengths
Those who give me inspiration
I'll afford them time with pleasure
Those who lift my spirits up
You deserve my attention
I'll not wait for tea given in resentment
I'll do me with glee and be happy
I'll have no unrealistic expectations
No thought shall cross my mind

I will be honest to myself
It's just a waste of time

'55' WOW !!

Fifty-five, that just don't look right
How and when did that number come about?
Take ten from that
Forty-five is about right
Time has been doing its thing whilst I was doing mine
How and when can I reconcile myself?
My life now fifty-five
When my mind says forty-five
I've got ten years' worth of catching up to do
Got to get the to-do list planned and rush through
The days and nights all merge into one
My dreams, my passions have only just begun
To make an appearance to the outer sphere
An appearance which is sparse and rare
Many rain clouds washed away the debris of the past years
Tornadoes came and went
Uncovering much needed challenges
That I can do and I will do
I will believe in the true pure strength of me
Inspiring my vision to be the best version of me
Now fifty-five, blessed and healthy

WHILST WE ARE HERE

Whilst we are here
Have we searched our hearts
For our true and intended purpose?
In pursuant of this journey, the road can be extremely rough
Unveiling unexpected revelations
Such an endeavour is very tough
But worth the impending rollercoaster ride
Good luck to all who step on that train
Blessings in abundance wait for the brave
Who are willing to search their mind and soul
For precious nuggets of gold
We all have this within us
It's there for us to find
So take the pill of fortitude
And shut the door behind you

LORD GIVE ME STRENGTH

Lord, give me strength to do what's right
Without the need for a fight
Give me words, the inspiring touch
That calms the spirit and gains the trust
Show the love and peace within
Not shouting and giving in
Tell the truth, no matter how hard
Letting my words be heard and healing grasped
Let a new understanding be reached by both
A new beginning and insight into who we are
And where we will go
Let no harsh words reach the ear
Of anyone too young to hear
The trauma of the adult family sphere
Blessed are the ones who take the time to listen
And are prepared to take selfless lessons
To replace what's really missing

REFRESH

Refresh my memory once again
What was it I'm supposed to do
What is it I am to say
Refresh my memory once again
What's the life I said I would have
The things I said I would always love
My writing, drawing, my self-love
The things I said I would put right
Hopefully by the end of the night
Refresh my memory once again
Play that song I'd dance to way back then
You know the one that made me jump and prance
Wiggle my hips
Oh I love to dance
Drop the beat
I remember now I am back on track
I remember how to do the things I'm supposed to
I remember how to say I love you

LIFE ON LOCKDOWN

It's the strength of your mind and heart
That counts and matters
When times get tough and rough
When it's you and yours that you are facing every day
Unable to hide behind what you would be doing all day
The things you said that once mattered
Have now been taken away
Exposing and revealing what you had hidden away
Now, time, there is abundance here
Time is the master of your fears
The master of your creative eyes and ears
Listen to the whispers loud and clear
Change your directions, ambitions and cares
And when it's all over and you emerge into the light
Remember the things you carefully considered
And chose to put right
Remember the pain of change
So you don't go there ever again
Remember to remain the improved version
Not the same
Now that you've had time to consider plans and set them in motion
A stripped-back purer authentic person called you
Not thrown to caution
I am the walking glory, the new me
A mission-driven human being
Whatever I want that to be

PARK OF DISCOVERY

In my park of discovery, I am alone
Alone with you, the keeper of my soul
I cannot hide
My body laid bare everything I have said, done, I do despair

In this park of discovery
I have uncovered the meaning of me
Why I came to be and why I am so
Blessed and happy to feel comfort in your spiritual hold

In my park of discovery, many times
Things have come to pass
People, places put out to grass
Like a big oak tree, there are many branches of me
Seen and yet to be seen

In my park of discovery
I am vulnerable and scared
Though protected by angels of life
Willing to step forward in times of trouble and strife

In my park of discovery
The beautiful flowers are many to see
They really speak to me
They show how birthing a new me
Can be a collage of vibrant energy

In my park of discovery
The flow of streams are endless

Meandering through valleys
Watering the mindfulness of the soul

In my park of discovery
I meet rocks and stones
They hinder the path that I stroll

But I know there are better days to come
So I pray for better days
They are coming real soon

Because in my park of discovery
Any hurt, pain and suffering
Are short-lived
As nature always revives all that is good

HOW MANY TIMES?

How many times have you gone to tell a story?
Just how many times, the words, they've failed you?
How many times have I put pen to paper
Not saying what really matters?
Just how many times I meant to say I love you
But my pride got in the way?
Unable to say those healing words, my fears came out to play

Just how many times have I meant to put my arms around you
To show I care and keep you close?
Just how many times have I meant to say I'm sorry?
Just how many times?

If I were brave enough to do and say the things
That matter most of all
Maybe I wouldn't feel so flawed
My fears were stronger
Than a compelling reason to take action
In so doing, I said nothing at all
I walked back my vulnerability
I did tell you I am flawed
So now, I'm on a healing journey
I feel safe enough to say
God gave me the gift of love
And I will make the time to say
I love you all so much
In such a very special way

GIVE ME

Give me an idea that I can run with
Something constructive and personal to me
Question my ideals, my reasoning and fortitude
My ambition, and consider my credulous position in life
Give me substance to feed the mind, shape
And mould creative energy
Seeping through the porous gateways of the earth
Showing, exposing what life is worth
The value of such is so subjective
What is precious to you could be another's nightmare
Give me a golden opportunity
To make a change worth mentioning
On another day, not for self or personal gain
Give me an extension of time
To make amends and do what is right in God's sight
This cannot be done overnight
Time, oh, time, we think we have plenty
How deluded sleepwalkers we've become
So pinch yourself out of sleep
And create the memories you want to keep

AM I GRATEFUL

Am I grateful or am I telling myself a lie?
Trying to smooth over the cracks and not cry
Am I really grateful or is it a lie so small
Or is it increasing in size?
Am I grateful or am I on repeat
Saying it over again
Just to keep my peace?
Am I grateful for what is seen and unseen?
Am I really grateful?
Am I telling myself my life has just begun?
Let me list my gratitudes one by one
I've turned the page
I have listed not even one
Why am I finding this so hard to do?
'Cause I am telling myself this ain't true
You're finding reasons to complain
Unconsciously sabotaging you
Instead of playing the forgiveness game
Forgive yourself for what's said and done
Forgive others too
Now start writing gratitude number one
It's all up to you
I am grateful to be alive today
I am grateful for my life
I am grateful to be able to breathe again and
To be a mother and a wife
I am grateful for my family and friends
I am grateful for health and strength

I am grateful that I am clothed and have food to eat
I am grateful for not sleeping on the park bench
I am grateful for my mum and dad
I am grateful that I have three beautiful children
I am grateful that I had experienced love
I am grateful that I can write
I am grateful for the universal blessing
I am grateful that God thinks I am all right
Now you have lifted off the runway of gratitude
Strap in, hold on tight
With an abundance of g-force
Taking your breath away
With grace and mercy accompanying on the flight
You will be grateful for so much more in this precious life

THE PURGE

Have you wrestled with your demons?
Have you FaceTimed with yourself?
Talked and talked and reasoned
Purged your thoughts and searched for meanings
Seeing light at the end of your meeting
Have you dug deep inside
And got out things that want to hide?
Gone into every crevice
Searching for things that will poison?
Seen stuff that is holding you back
Suppressing, depressing and not letting you thrive
Emerging from the box you're in?
Have you really told yourself the truth?
You know the good the bad and the ugly within
Been elated on the good
Remorseful of the bad and accepting of the ugly?
Put away the should have, would have and could have?
Now that you have done all that
Have you forgiven yourself, your friends and your family
And allowed yourself to be?
This is the season for your time to grow and smile
Don't linger in the past
Take down the veil you hide behind
Let greatness take the stand
Knowing not all that glitters is pure gold
But it is the truth at last

YOU

It's not a bad thing to spend time with yourself
With no one, just the air you breathe keeping you company
My senses sharpened
I can respond to how I am feeling
In the back of my mind, I am conscious of someone listening
Watching to see what I am doing
Let go of those fears, just relax and be you
Breathe deep and follow through
My head is full with lots of stuff
I am really not sure what to do with
Contemplating whether or not to share me
With another human being
How do I want to make a difference in life
To myself, my family and my friends
To all that matters in the end
I've critique so far, there is room for much improvement
I have loved and lost the battle of wills
Living in ignorance I can see
Has contributed to many failing families
So educate, read and listen, too
Wholesome words of truth
Be the best of life you can be
Be you, be mum, be a good wife and friend
Be happy, be true to all you meet and greet
Don't worry what others say
They will laugh and plot a downfall anyway
There will be sniggers, smears and criticism, too
Don't watch that there is much to do

A powerful purpose you have before you
A bold story to be told
With blessed assurance, it will be done
Your task, you must complete
Don't procrastinate because time does not wait
Just open all the floodgates

ME

I do not aspire to be anyone but myself
And that is the stumbling block
To be me is what?
And when I arrive, to whom
Do I present?
Why question the being you are?
Is it worth the inquisition?
As I said
I don't aspire to be anyone but me
Who that is
Just wait and see

GOD'S PLAN

When God has a plan
No problem is too great to work through
Many roads to be taken
A course with many in mind
I am no better than you today
And I cannot see how things are to be
But I trust that wherever he takes me
It's where I should be

The Light

Nor does anyone light a lamp and put it under a basket, but on a lampstand, and it gives light to all in the house.

Matthew 5:15

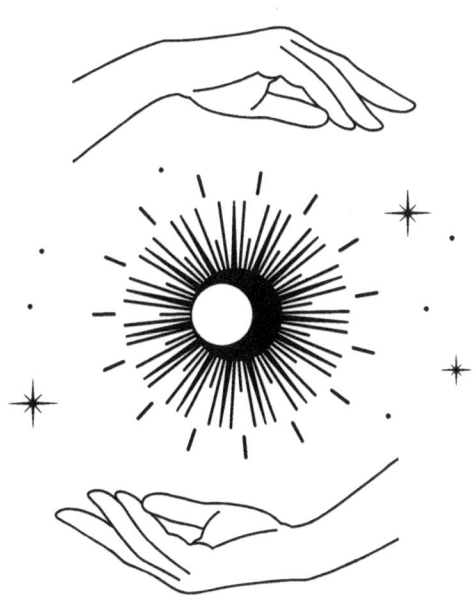

BEAUTIFUL BIRD

Fly by, my beautiful bird
Spread your wings and sing
Fly by gracious being
Survey the world you're in
Breathe, exhale, don't give in
Pressures will come freely

Fly by, you courageous creature
Pick out your colours from the rainbow
Dip your beak in the stream
See the reflection of your dreams
In crystal, ultra-high definition

Fear not the path your flight will take
It matters not the plans you make
Enjoy the ride of your life past, present and future
Soar high, dive deep into the wonders of this world
Capture all there is to know

If failure is, in spite of persistence
Don't panic, just call for a little assistance
The universe is bound to honour all great efforts made
Despite your demeanour
Given time, rest and a period of reflection
Your lessons will be learnt
You'll fly by again, you beautiful bird

NIGHT OUT

A night out with friends is so revealing
Laughter and gaiety prevail indeed
Eating, chatting, belly laughs for all
Enjoying the company right across the board
Each has a story to tell
Nothing too heavy
Appreciating each other
For what we all bring to the table of life
And what we are drinking
Whether it be the wine from heaven
Or the devil's brew
We accept we are all human
Not aloof and nobody's fool
I say thank you for all that's said and done
It was no coincidence
It was meant to happen

GLITCH

Write to release the glitch in your life
Tell all to smooth out the flaws
Make a pathway to healthy living and
Right the wrongs in your songs
No more melancholy woes
Just let the truth of you be told
How it's beauty in life you seek
Just realise that the glitch in your life is
Only temporary
For it's you alone who controls the delete button, the eraser
A new and welcoming blank sheet
Put life into your words
And shimmering watercolour in your prints
Make history in the making
And fun in the love of your world
Peace be with you all the time
Bring out what you have inside
Clear out the glitches
Have me in stitches with belly laughs and tears
Paint pictures of your happiness so I will smile all the time

MEMORIES

In case I don't remember
Tell me it's only memories, that's all we have
In case I don't remember
Remind me of all the things we said and loved
In case I don't remember
Tell me stupid tales of joy and sadness
In case I don't remember

Remind me to laugh, sing and dance
Put a sunbeam smile on that beautiful face of mine
Remind me, look at me deeply
I'm still in there
Can you see me?
Help me to remember me
And if I don't remember
Please be kind to me
Hold my hand and sing sweetly
Gently bring me back to reality
Hope this will not be my destiny
But if this is to be
Please be patient with me
For nobody knows what lies ahead
So create the memories you want instead
And not a life that is full of regrets

CALM

When everything is calm, no worries about
And all is going well
Do you dare to break the spell?
Pay attention to the realm that brought you here
These feelings, the smell, the aura
The space or place that found the love, the order
Be amazed by what you attract
Invite yourself in
Attend the event with much vigour and passion
Seize the moment and stay in the blessing
The feeling is true, it's you
Keep believing in what you deserve
And what is for you will be for you

NOISE

Learn to tune out the noise
It is a sure way not to avoid what you should do
And then recoil
Test your ability to remain focused and calm
Even when things around you seem to be crashing down
Learn to tune out the voices
That distract you from the path
That bank on you to quit, turn around and run fast
Switch-up the vision that says you won't make it
That freezes your mind and puts fear in it
Learn to block out the increasing volume
Shut it down and turn it around
God never made you to have your face in the ground

FEET

My feet have taken me a long way
Far and near, to the valley and the bays
I've walked into the light and leapt from the darkness
My steps have led me to happiness and to lay down in sorrow
They've rested in the clear waters
Soaking away the months, days and years
They've danced to songs of life
They've guided me through dreams, ambitions and desires
My wants, my needs and inspirations
Your feet, they have a life of their own
If crushed, stepped on or tried to be controlled
It's funny how they say, 'Hey ho! Let's go'
Turning on their heels if faced with oppression
Taking to the streets without hesitation
A vessel that possess divine energy
Making grounding very powerful, indeed
Helping to manage your desires
And bring them into conscious being
Walk the path your feet will take you
Embrace the journey of their will
Trust your feet—they know your guilty pleasures
One step, two steps, three steps or more
Tentatively feeling for that open door
One leap to freedom, to life's engaging sights
And anything enhancing the soul
Soaking up the will of the dance floor
Unapologetically, you put them through their paces
Ignoring their instructions

Intuitively signalling for you
To march along, stamp along and run
Pressing ahead with no time to consider in depth your journey
Stop, listen, take care and rest
Take time and pay attention
There are many lessons before bed
Those feet are unashamedly yours
So whenever and wherever they may take you
Say thank you and adore those precious feet of yours

SPACE

I can't say I'm happy
But I can say I'm in a happier space
I can go to bed smiling, laughing to myself
Content that all is well
It is well now and will be for the future
You're blessed and favoured by all
In more ways than one
Even from the unlikely one
So I am thankful, grateful
And humbled by the experience
Recognising the wealth within the well
All is well, I say
No more worry from today

LIFE LIGHTS

When God turns your lights off in the world we now live in
When the light he gave you to shine burns dimly
Or not at all
Did you use the opportunities to show what he created
And made within?
Your choices in life
Did they reflect the totality of your worth?
The gifts and all his blessings?

Isn't that a question!
So whenever you have the time
Or opportunity presents itself
Let your candle burn brightly in every given moment
Give thanks and praise for everything

And everyone you meet
Smile broadly like the sun, the moon and the stars
Grab life and laugh hard
'Cause when God turns those lights out
There will be no flicker, no flame
The candle oil will run dry and cannot be reclaimed
So burn, burn bright here on Earth
Shine right through the maze of everyone
Let all see who you are
The child of God, authentic in every way
Now let's not pretend you were perfect in all your ways
'Cause perfection is only found in the One we praise
Love truly and deeply

Do the best that you can do
Be honest and kind and helpful all the time
Show your fellow man how to love and have a really good time
'Cause when those lights go out
You hope to leave behind
A legacy of goodwill
That transcends all time

EVERYTHING

Everything I've asked for
You have given it to me
In time I can say I've received it eventually
Waiting on you, you've never let me down
I can honestly say
I've got my pay someway, somehow
Everything I've asked for
I've received indeed
Learning to trust you was difficult for me
Wanting things to happen my way
I couldn't see
My faith had been tested continuously
You shaped my life for the better
I can see
Everything you've done now and forever
You have done it just for me

THE BRAVE

You know you're braver than you look
Go on, push through
You know you're braver than you look
You're stronger than you think
You are a goddess, a queen
An embodiment of love supreme
Earth has given you all you need
To dream, to succeed and achieve
To conquer the fears of failure
To dig deeper to the heart of euphoria
And take your rightful place on the throne
Of total self-respect
You know self-worth, self-love
The glow that makes you who you are
Don't be rattled by the chatter
You are the monarchy of you
The sole ruler of your being
God created you, His queen
So embrace your crown, wear it with pride
The angels are sent to protect and guide
If you dispute this analogy of you
Then I surely beg to differ
'Cause the universe wouldn't let me pen these words
If it didn't speak to me first

THE CANVAS

My sight fails in more ways than one
It fails to see the blank canvas
Beneath the vibrant colours
Hides the smudges of indiscretion
The fingerprints of truth
And the DNA of blood, sweat and tears
That has been concealed by the canvas over many years
Now a new year and new day, choice is given
What do I choose to believe and see?
It is ultimately my decision
That's entirely up to me
So I paint a picture of encouragement
Self-revealing, self-evident
In self-belief
I question: does the canvas really capture me?
At dawn, I breathe in fresh, clean air
And my sight connects to see patterns unfolding
As thoughts race through my mind
I close my eyes and embrace the sun with a smile
The senses on my body wake, then tickle my abilities
A light breeze calmly whispers to thee
Saying, I am the great I Am; be still and listen to Me
I have given you a new beginning
A brief for a new painting
Trust your instincts, your intuition
And your spiritual capabilities
Your sight has now fully returned
By grace, you've been reborn with new vision

You are not what you've been
Nor what you have previously learned
Stay true to yourself
Be good to yourself
Stick to My brief
And paint your canvas with strong conviction
Let Me be your eyes for you
I will take your hand and guide you
Trust in Me and you will be forgiven
For all that canvas has kept hidden
All the smudges of indiscretions
Will no longer be a binding authority
Because with Me, there will always be many new beginnings
A new day, a new way to express My will
And my perfect vision

WATER

Turn your back on what you've seen
Take a walk to the ravine
Wash your feet in the stream
Dip your courage in new scenes
Make intrinsic connections with numerous beings
Strip naked and shower in a rainfall of your blessings
Wash away what is not pressing
There's power in the water
Cleansing the skin and the mind deep within
Oxygenating the weak and the fading
Giving life to the shrivelled
Energising the steps we are taking
The feeling is so fresh and oh so invigorating
There's power in the water
When heated, it boils away life's toxic gems
Trying to cling to our souls
As the temperature falls
The freeze temporarily holds our woes
Over time, we soaked up life's dirty water
Then failed to use all our natural filters
Our instincts, gut feelings the faint voice we hear and ignore
When there's a meltdown, we have a breakdown
Shedding tears for collection
There is hope to start all over when you wash with the water
We see the drips of our choices upon reflection
Turn your back on what you have been
And in time you will see
The blessings in the awesome power of the water

NATURE IS PERFECTLY IMPERFECT

Nature is perfectly imperfect
Imperfections are there for a reason
To shape, to hold, to remould
To create a reaction, to start a conversation
Thus reasoning the hows and the whys
Fostering a healthy appreciation
Respecting the differences, alliances and boundaries
The symbiotic truth that exists
Challenges the physical and moral compass
Of the human mind
It's beautiful to see an awesome body of vibrant energy
A conscious being with endless intricate networks
Of discovery and possibilities
I am perfectly imperfect
A form unique to me alone
Being at one with my soul
Accepting the perplexing, however things come about
Appreciating the uniqueness of what the world has on offer
A deep breath, I take in
I close my eyes to relive the pictures of the blessings
I see each morning
Everyday I pray to see again
The universal wonders displayed to all men and women
I gasp in amazement
And cry tears of joy
That God's creations are so perfectly imperfect
We're so blessed and able to enjoy
I am humbled at the thought that God still loves me
Knowing I'm so perfectly imperfect

ABOUT THE AUTHOR

Mecheal Elizabeth is a British author, poet and mother on a spiritually lead journey of rediscovery and healing. Through her poetry and storytelling, Mecheal shares her light with the world in the hopes that the divinity that guides her through her trauma and into her power is awakened within her readers.

ACKNOWLEDGEMENTS

I dedicate this piece of my soul to the Lord. This is my personal sacrifice. I thank you for my spiritual awakening. I am grateful for the gift of life loving God, the wonderful healer and protector. May I always be aware of myself because awareness of my ignorance is the beginning of wisdom. Lead me to where I need to be because when anyone walks with you, they make it to their final destination. I call on You, Lord, that you bless my dreams which I have placed before you. Remind me to continually consult You each step of the way, taking my steps into the unknown with Your guidance and protection, remaining truly faithful and letting nothing and no one dim the light You have placed inside me. May grace and humility be instilled in me.

A special shoutout to my precious children. I am blessed with three beautiful souls. I cannot remember life without them, and I love them so much. With all the trials and tribulations, they make me proud to be their mother. They inspire me to be a better version of myself, pushing me and challenging me to do more.

I wish to say a special thank you to Daniella, who was divinely sent to me. Without her, my poetry would not have a stage.

Lastly, to my family and friends who kept me going and who support this journey: God bless you all.

All is Well.

Love, Mecheal

Conscious Dreams
PUBLISHING

Transforming diverse writers
into successful published authors

www.consciousdreamspublishing.com

authors@consciousdreamspublishing.com

Let's connect

www.ingramcontent.com/pod-product-compliance
Lightning Source LLC
Chambersburg PA
CBHW040242130526
44590CB00049B/4172